Other Books by the Author

The Bread of Life
Fundamental Bible Study Course

Seeking His Fellowship

Is the Bible True?
If So, Which One?

The Antichrist

Spiritual Warfare

Road To Hell
Acts 2

Road To Hell
Acts 2

By Chaplain Ted L. Warmack, D.D.

Bible Believer's Outreach Inc. Publishing
9835 Woodland Hills Way Tallahassee, FL 32309

Copyright 2013
By Ted L. Warmack
All rights reserved

PUBLISHER'S NOTE
Scripture quotations are from the text of the Authorized King James Version of the Bible. Any deviations are not intentional.

No portion of this publication may be reproduced by any means without the expressed written consent of the author.

1st Printing December 2015

ISBN
978-1-942050-03-2

Dedication

This booklet is dedicated to all those who love the Lord, believe the Book and seek the truth. May it be a valuable tool in opening the eyes of those who have been deceived by the heresy of water regeneration.

Contents

Chapter	Page
Preface	v
1. Heresy	1
2. Salvation In Acts	9
3. Which Baptism?	23
4. Rightly Dividing	29
Bible Salvation	40

Preface

Since the Church Age began, the powers of darkness have worked endlessly to keep people from being saved and to then confuse and divide those who did become born again.

The Devil knows his end is the lake of fire and his present desire is to take as many with him as he can. The easiest way to achieve this goal is to deceive people into following a false Gospel and then die unsaved while believing they are saved.

This has been easy to achieve as few bother to study the Bible or search the Scriptures as commanded (II Tim. 2:15, John 5:39, KJV). The result is a divided band of believers with many trusting in their own works and the wrong way to salvation.

It is a sad thing to think of all those who will end up in Hell because they failed to study and seek the truth themselves and instead trusted their soul to what another said. This booklet reflects the burden I have for those. May it help those blinded by false gospels and lead them to Jesus Christ.

Chapter 1

Heresy

"There is a way which seemeth right unto a man, but the end thereof are the ways of death."
Proverbs 14:12

Never before has the New Testament Church landscape been so saturated with heresy and false doctrine regarding salvation than in these last days before the return of our Lord Jesus Christ.

As any serious student of the Bible knows, nearly all of these heresies come from the New Testament books of Matthew, Acts, and Hebrews. **While most of these teachings are indeed a truth in another dispensation or time period they are not part of the true Gospel of Jesus Christ and therefore do not apply to our salvation today as easily proved with Scripture.**

Since all false Gospels presently being taught are

under a curse, they are sending many to hell daily (Gal. 1:8). The Apostle Paul made this abundantly clear after telling us what the one and only true gospel is (I Cor. 15:1-4) We will look at this in more detail later.

This lesson is dealing with today's most commonly taught heresies that come from the book of Acts Chapter Two. I can safely say that more people die and go to Hell trusting in verses taken out of context in Acts than any other book in the Bible. Also, that more die and go to Hell in Acts 2:38 than any other one chapter and verse.

There are three primary false teachings that originate in Acts 2 so we will look at each one. First, let's look at the two heresys taught on the Holy Ghost and tongues. Let's rely on what the Bible says on these subjects and not just what we have heard nor been taught.

Acts 2:1 *"And when the day of Pentecost was fully come, they were all with one accord in one place. [2] And suddenly there came a sound from heaven as of a rushing mighty wind, and it filled all the house where they were sitting. [3] And there appeared unto them cloven tongues like as of fire,* *and it sat upon each of them. [4] And they were all filled with the Holy Ghost, and began to speak with other tongues, as the Spirit gave them utterance. [5] And there were dwelling at Jerusalem Jews, devout men, out of every nation under heaven. [6] Now when this was noised abroad, the multitude came together, and were confounded, because that every man heard them speak in his own language. [7] And they were all amazed and marvelled, saying one to another, Behold, are not all these which speak Galilaeans? [8] And how hear we every man in our own tongue, wherein we were born? [9] Parthians, and Medes, and Elamites, and the dwellers in Mesopotamia, and in Judaea, and Cappadocia, in Pontus, and Asia, [10] Phrygia, and Pamphylia, in Egypt, and in the parts of Libya about Cyrene, and strangers of Rome, Jews and proselytes, [11] Cretes and Arabians, we do hear them speak in our tongues the wonderful works of God."*

Holy Ghost And Tongues: The teachings in question are that:

(1) The initial evidence of receiving the Holy Ghost is speaking in tongues.

(2) That speaking in tongues is necessary to be saved. **Both are wrong!**

Let's examine the Scripture and let the Bible clear up this mess! First, note that in Acts 2:1 on the day of Pentecost that "THEY" were in one accord and in one place. Continuing from the very beginning of chapter One, we learn that the "they" referred to are the apostles! Then in verse four, they (the apostles) spoke in other tongues.

They spoke in "other tongues" (other languages) not any unknown tongues. No one other than the apostles spoke in tongues, however everyone understood in their own language!

Moreover, the "cloven tongues" appeared to them, then they were filled with the Holy Ghost. "They," the apostles!

Note also the "initial evidence" of the Holy Ghost was a **rushing mighty wind,** not anyone speaking in tongues as you have heard some say! Many among the multitudes that were present that day, about three thousand (Acts 2:41) were saved. Those did not speak in tongues (other languages); only the apostles did!

So, obviously, Acts 2 cannot be used to prove speaking in tongues is the evidence of receiving the Holy Ghost. The apostles were already saved when this took place.

Neither can one prove with Scripture that speaking in tongues is necessary for salvation. It is simply not in the Bible

We do not want to spend a lot of time on the tongues issue as it is the subject of another work and we prefer to remain on the subject of salvation and the main subject of this book which is Acts 2:38.

Salvation today does not require any kind of "works" or anything you have to do, such as speaking in tongues or any physical action other than receiving Jesus Christ through prayer, and trusting His shed Blood as payment for your sins. (Eph. 2:8, Rom. 10 9-10, Titus 3:5). We will deal with this in more detail later as we proceed.

The next false teaching that is taught from Acts 2 is a very controversial subject among believers. However, it is always simple to find the truth when you examine Scripture with Scripture in the proper context. Let's see where that leads us.

The Road to Hell, Acts 2

Water Regeneration: Water Baptism is being taught as necessary for salvation by most modern day denominations. The majority of these cite Acts 2:38 to justify this teaching. Even though there are other plans of salvation in Acts and Water baptism is not taught as part of new covenant salvation anywhere in the Pauline Epistles, many still hold this position.

What a shock for some to hear that statement! Well, you now have two choices. You can just believe what you have heard and what you want to believe, or you can continue reading and find out what the Bible really says on this subject examined in the proper context.

I challenge you to stay with us and if not convinced when finished, write and give us your verses to the contrary! Give them in the proper context of course! However, I guarantee you will have little on which to stand when we are finished but shifting sand. Although, you are welcome to try!

This lesson is incredibly simple, however there is a lot of ground to cover so let's get started. First of all, we need to spend some time in the book of Acts and show how Acts 2:38 could not possibly be the plan of salvation for our time!

It will shock some but the fact is, no one was ever saved according to Acts 2:38 anywhere in the Bible except for those few Jews which the Apostle Peter was addressing there on that day! You might want to read that again!

Moreover, none of the apostles were baptized according to Acts 2:38 (in the name of Jesus)! If Acts 2:38 was even a part of the plan of salvation for today the Apostle Paul would have told us so in the thirteen books of the Bible he wrote (the Pauline Epistles). After all he was the apostle to the Gentiles (Gal. 2:8) and God's chosen vessel to spread the Gospel of Jesus Christ to the world!

To understand what was going on in Acts 2, you must understand, that with respect to salvation, the book of Acts is a transitional book. It transitions between the Old Testament way to salvation by works and salvation in this age through faith in the shed blood of Jesus Christ (plus nothing)! It is a free gift with no works of any kind necessary. *"For by grace are ye saved through faith; and that not of yourselves: it it is the gift of God: [9] Not of works, lest any man should boast."* (Eph. 2:8-9)

And: *"Not by works of righteousness which we have done, but according to his mercy he saved us, by the washing of regeneration, and renewing of the Holy Ghost; [6] Which he shed on us abundantly through Jesus Christ our Saviour."* (Titus 3:5-7)

Notice no water baptism, and no speaking in tongues for salvation here but let's take it all in order.

Since there are several different ways to salvation in the book of Acts (which we will examine) it is hard to understand why one (Acts 2:38) would be picked over any of the several others; especially since there were no Gentiles involved in Acts 2:38 and because it soundly contradicts the teachings on salvation throughout the New Testament Pauline Epistles!

So, first we will look at the several different ways people were saved in Acts; then we will deal with the other verses taken out of context to teach this heresy. Stay with us as we move toward the true way to salvation.

Chapter 2

Salvation in Acts

"Search the scriptures; for in them ye think ye have eternal life: and they are they which testify of me." John 5:39

This chapter will show the progression of the Book of Acts as it transitions from the Old to the New Covenant with respect to salvation. We will look at the several different ways to salvation found in Acts and the likely reason God chose this course to reveal the real way to salvation under the New Testament Covenant.

It will not be a difficult study if you believe the Bible rather than what you have heard or been told.

[36] "Therefore let all the house of Israel know assuredly, that God hath made that same Jesus, whom ye have crucified, both Lord and Christ.

[37] Now when they heard this, they were pricked in their heart, and said unto Peter and to the rest of the apostles, Men and brethren, what shall we do? [38] Then Peter said unto them, Repent, and be baptized every one of you in the name of Jesus Christ for the remission of sins, and ye shall receive the gift of the Holy Ghost." (Acts 2:36-38)

Verse 38 is very plain here and indicates salvation by repenting, and being baptized in the name of Jesus Christ for the remission of sins. Some say that when these Jews were pricked in their hearts, that was an indication they had first believed and were therefore saved before being baptized.

We will not go there because it is not necessary to prove our point. Rather, as we will accept this as the way of salvation for those Jews (and them alone) that got the message in Acts two and believed. We will also show that this was only one of several ways to salvation in this transitional book. So now, let's have a look at some of those other ways people were saved in the book of Acts.

[14]"Now when the apostles which were at Jerusalem heard that Samaria had received the word of God, they sent unto them Peter and John:

[15] Who, when they were come down, prayed for them, that they might receive the Holy Ghost: [16] (For as yet he was fallen upon none of them: only they were baptized in the name of the Lord Jesus. [17] Then laid they their hands on them, and they received the Holy Ghost". (Acts 8:14-17) (Underline emphasis ours throughout.)

There are two good points here. First, these had heard the word, been prayed for and been baptized in Jesus' name but that did not save them as it did the Jews in Acts 2:38! Secondly, **They were not saved until Peter and John laid their hands on them!** This is a new way to salvation in Acts. Baptism here but no salvation resulted!

Later in Chapter eight we find the first conversion in Acts by faith, with no laying on of hands, and no speaking in tongues, and no water baptism until after being saved. This is the way we are saved today. The Ethiopian eunuch heard Jesus Christ preached to him and was saved by faith, believing that He was the Son of God. Then he was baptized after being saved as a testimony of his conversion!

[36]"And as they went on their way, they came unto a certain water: and the eunuch said, See,

here is water; what doth hinder me to be baptized? [37] And Philip said, If thou believest with all thine heart, thou mayest. And he answered and said, I believe that Jesus Christ is the Son of God. [38] And he commanded the chariot to stand still: and they went down both into the water, both Philip and the eunuch; and he baptized him." (Acts 8:36-38)

Understand that Philip would never have baptized the eunuch if he had not been saved first! The water baptism was (and is now) a physical picture of the Spiritual baptism of the Holy Ghost. It was not (neither is it now) part of his salvation, but rather a type or picture of the salvation which had already taken place, reflecting a death, a burial and a resurrection!

So, in eight chapters of Acts you already have three paths to salvation. Let's look further.

Here we have Saul (later Paul) who had met the Lord Jesus on the road to Damascus (and lost his eyesight as a result) being ministered to.

[10]"And there was a certain disciple at Damascus, named Ananias; and to him said the Lord in a vision, Ananias. And he said, Behold, I am here,

Lord. [11] And the Lord said unto him, Arise, and go into the street which is called Straight, and enquire in the house of Judas for one called Saul, of Tarsus: for, behold, he prayeth, [12] And hath seen in a vision a man named Ananias coming in, and putting his hand on him, that he might receive his sight. [13] Then Ananias answered, Lord, I have heard by many of this man, how much evil he hath done to thy saints at Jerusalem: [14] And here he hath authority from the chief priests to bind all that call on thy name. [15] <u>But the Lord said unto him, Go thy way: for he is a chosen vessel unto me, to bear my name before the Gentiles, and kings, and the children of Israel:</u> [16] For I will shew him how great things he must suffer for my name's sake. [17] And Ananias went his way, and entered into the house; and putting his hands on him said, Brother Saul, the Lord, even Jesus, that appeared unto thee in the way as thou camest, hath sent me, <u>that thou mightest receive thy sight, and be filled with the Holy Ghost. [18] And immediately there fell from his eyes as it had been scales: and he received sight forthwith, and arose, and was baptized.</u>" (Acts 9:10-18)

Salvation came to Saul, along with his sight being restored when one appointed and empowered by God laid hands on him. **Notice he was saved before being baptized!** It's about to get even more interesting. Moving on to Acts 10.

[44]"While Peter yet spake these words, the Holy Ghost fell on all them which heard the word. [45] And they of the circumcision which believed were astonished, as many as came with Peter, because that on the Gentiles also was poured out the gift of the Holy Ghost. [46] For they heard them speak with tongues, and magnify God. Then answered Peter, [47] Can any man forbid water, that these should not be baptized, which have received the Holy Ghost as well as we? [48] And he commanded them to be baptized in the name of the Lord." (Acts 10:44-48)

Number four! Well, it is really getting interesting now! **Notice, the Holy Ghost revealed to Peter that not only were these saved before water baptism, but that some Gentiles were saved as well. They also spoke in tongues (which is a sign for the Jews present because the Jew requires a sign, I Cor. 1:22).**

Before it gets too confusing, let's look at where we are so far.

Salvation in Acts

1) Acts 2:38 Saved by repenting and **being baptized** in Jesus' name.

2) Acts 8:14-17 Saved by the **laying on of hands** after baptism which did not save.

3) Acts 8:36-38: Saved by faith the same as we are now. Baptized after being saved.

4) Acts 9:10-18 Saved by laying on of hands and then baptized after being saved.

5) Acts 10:44-48 Saved by faith, speaking in tongues and then baptized after being saved!

Notice the different elements in each of the five ways to salvation! Like we said earlier, Acts is a transitional book. It is taking you somewhere so hang on! There's more!

[13]"And he shewed us how he had seen an angel in his house, which stood and said unto him, Send men to Joppa, and call for Simon, whose surname is Peter; [14] Who shall tell thee words, whereby thou and all thy house shall be saved. [15] And as I began to speak, the Holy Ghost fell on them, as on us at the beginning. [16]"Then remembered I the

word of the Lord, how that he said, *John indeed baptized with water; but ye shall be baptized with the Holy Ghost. [17] Forasmuch then as God gave them the like gift as he did unto us, who believed on the Lord Jesus Christ; what was I, that I could withstand God?"* (Acts 11:13-17) Notice no tongues here.

Peter said these got saved from believing like he did. What happened to Acts 2:38 and the water baptism? John told them a greater baptism than his water baptism was coming and that was baptism of the Holy Ghost! (Matt. 3:11) Baptism of the Holy Ghost is the real thing. That's the one you must have! Peter is recognizing the difference here. Number five!

[6]"And the apostles and elders came together for to consider of this matter. [7]And when there had been much disputing, Peter rose up, and said unto them, Men and brethren, ye know how that a good while ago God made choice among us, that the Gentiles by my mouth should hear the word of the gospel, and believe. [8] And God, which knoweth the hearts, bare them witness, giving them the Holy Ghost, even as he did unto us; [9] And put no difference between us and them, purifying their

hearts by faith. [10] Now therefore why tempt ye God, to put a yoke upon the neck of the disciples, which neither our fathers nor we were able to bear? [11] But we believe that through the grace of the Lord Jesus Christ we shall be saved, even as they." (Acts 15:6-11)

Remember that this is the same Peter who in Acts 2:38 told some Jews (who just realized they had crucified their Saviour) to be baptized in the name of Jesus Christ to receive the Holy Ghost. He has since had his eyes opened and is now saying salvation comes through FAITH! Further, he points out that the apostles were saved as they were, by faith without the yoke of water baptism which is a work, not faith. Once again....

[25]"And at midnight Paul and Silas prayed, and sang praises unto God: and the prisoners heard them. [26] And suddenly there was a great earthquake, so that the foundations of the prison were shaken: and immediately all the doors were opened, and every one's bands were loosed. [27] And the keeper of the prison awaking out of his sleep, and seeing the prison doors open, he drew out his sword, and would have killed himself, supposing that the prisoners had been fled. [28]

But Paul cried with a loud voice, saying, Do thyself no harm: for we are all here. [29] Then he called for a light, and sprang in, and came trembling, and fell down before Paul and Silas, [30] And bought them out, and said, Sirs, what must I do to be saved? [31] And they said, Believe on the Lord Jesus Christ, and thou shalt be saved, and thy house." (Acts 16:25-31)

This is the first time someone in Acts has asked the direct question, *"what must I do to be saved?"* **The answer given is not be baptized, it is not do good works, it is not obey the commandments, it is not to do the sacraments or to go to church on the Sabbath, but rather BELIEVE! Believe on the Lord Jesus Christ and thou shall be saved! Got it?**

Both he and his family were saved and then baptized. They were not baptized as part of their salvation but <u>because</u> they had been saved. Once again; the water baptism was a physical picture of what had happened spiritually inside when they were baptized by the Holy Ghost and saved! More on this later!

Now the importance of the instruction to *"believe on the Lord Jesus Christ and thou shalt be saved...."*

can be weighed by who made the statement. Remember that Paul was the Apostle to the Gentiles (Rom. 11:13) and the chosen vessel to bring the new covenant of salvation by grace through faith to the world. You can trust what he said! Here is the last example from Acts.

[3]"And he said unto them, Unto what then were ye baptized? And they said, Unto John's baptism. [4] Then said Paul, John verily baptized with the baptism of repentance, saying unto the people that they should believe on him which should come after him, that is, on Christ Jesus." [5] When they heard this, they were baptized in the name of the Lord Jesus. 6 And when Paul had laid his hands upon them, the Holy Ghost came on them; and they spake with tongues, and prophesied. 7 And all the men were about twelve." (Acts 19:3-7)

Once again they believed and were saved by the laying on of hands by an apostle <u>after</u> baptism which <u>did not save</u> like in Acts eight. The difference here is that they spoke in tongues.

So let's sum up what we find in the Book of Acts. Acts 2:38 Saved by repenting and being **baptized** in Jesus' name.

The Road to Hell, Acts 2

Acts 8:14-17: Saved by the laying on of hands after baptism which did not save.

Acts 8:36-38: Saved by faith the same as we are now. Baptized after being saved.

Acts 9:10-18: Saved by laying on of **hands** before baptism.

Acts 10:44-48: Saved by faith, then spoke in tongues and was baptized after being saved!

Acts 11:13-17: Saved by faith, no water baptism.

Acts 16:25-3: Saved by faith before baptism.

Acts 19:3-7: Once again they were saved by the laying on of **hands** after baptism. The difference here is that they spoke in tongues after being saved.

What you have just read is people being saved under five different circumstances in Acts. **1)** Water baptism, **2)** laying on of hands, **3)** faith, **4)** faith with tongues, **5)** hands with tongues.

Notice that other than Acts 2:38 no one received the Holy Ghost and was saved by water baptism!

What a revelation! All were saved by faith, or the laying on of hands by God's anointed after hearing the word and believing.

One would naturally wonder why the Lord gave so many different circumstances under which people were saved and how in the world do we know the correct one for today. Which one should we choose?

Apparently, God was not ready to reveal the New Covenant of salvation (by grace through faith) in Acts 2 because He was still dealing with the Jews as a nation until Acts seven when they rejected Jesus Christ and stoned Steven. Then immediately (in chapter 8) the Gentile Ethiopia eunuch was saved by faith, as are we in this present day.

However, no one is saved in this present day by the apolostic power of "laying on of hands" or by speaking in tongues. Neither has anyone ever been saved by being baptized in the name of Jesus Christ for the remission of sins since Acts 2:38!

Now that we have seen the transition from salvation by water baptism to salvation by faith, let's examine some more proof that water baptism is **not** necessary for salvation.

The Road to Hell, Acts 2

Chapter 3

Which Baptism?

"One Lord, one faith, one baptism."
Ephesians 4:5

A good preacher friend of mine says the problem today is that every time someone hears the word baptism they think of water and when they hear water they think of baptism and neither is always true in the Bible.

Actually, there are seven baptisms in the Bible and not all are water! Well, how do we explain the verse **"One Lord, one faith, one baptism"** found in Ephesians 4:5? Let's look further as we peruse what John the Baptist said.

[11]"I indeed baptize you with water unto repentance: but he that cometh after me is mightier than I, whose shoes I am not worthy to bear: he

shall baptize you with the Holy Ghost, and with fire: 12 Whose fan is in his hand, and he will throughly purge his floor, and gather his wheat into the garner; but he will burn up the chaff with unquenchable fire." (Matt. 3:11-12)

Notice that there are three baptisms here: **Water, Holy Ghost and fire.** John, speaking of Jesus, indicates Jesus is bringing a better baptism than his water baptism! Since chaff is a type of sin or the ungodly (Ps. 1:4) and the baptism of fire is Hell (V12). The baptism of the Holy Ghost is the one you want! Not baptism of water or fire, but the one that puts you into HIM!

Would you rather be put in water or Hell physically, or put in Jesus Christ Spiritually? Not much of a choice there. Amen?

So, Ephesians Four says there is only one baptism, while Matthew 3:11 says there is three. Well, does the Bible contradict itself? Of course not! It simply means there is only one real, or saving baptism. Proof?

Watch this: *[12]"For as the body is one, and hath many members, and all the members of that one body, being many, are one body: so also is Christ. [13] For by one Spirit are we all baptized into one body, whether we be Jews or Gentiles, whether we be bond or free; and have been all made to drink into one Spirit."* (I Cor. 12:12-13)

The capital "S" in Spirit indicates the Holy Spirit. If you are saved, you are saved by being baptized into the body of Christ by the Holy Spirit, and not by water! Get that! The baptism you need is not one performed by some preacher but rather a Spiritual baptism by the Holy Ghost of God!

Now knowing what you have just read, would you rather have the baptism of water, the Holy Ghost baptism, or the baptism of fire? You will not have a problem saying "the Holy Ghost" if you believe the Bible!

Of course there are some other verses we must deal with, and we will; first let's firm up what we have already proved.

Here is some more proof (some of which we have already looked at) that water baptism does not save you. *"To him give all the prophets witness, that through his name whosoever believeth in him shall receive remission of sins."* (Acts 10:43) There is no water here for remission of sins; it's faith!

Yet another one showing salvation without water. *[44]"While Peter yet spake these words, the Holy Ghost fell on all them which heard the word... Can any man forbid water, that these should not be baptized, which have received the Holy Ghost as well as we?"* (Acts 10: 44&47) Saved first, then baptized second.

Verse 43 makes it plain that you are saved by believing in Christ, and then again in verse 44 you see those people were saved before they were baptized!!

This was the Holy Spirit showing Peter that the Old Testament Jewish water baptism was not required for salvation under the new covenant of salvation by grace through faith.

You have seen another good example of salvation before water baptism in Acts 8:37. The Ethiopian eunuch wanted to be baptized, but Phillip said: *"If thou believest with all thine heart, thou mayest.."*

Believe and be saved by the baptism of the Holy

Ghost, then get baptized in water! This serves as a picture of your salvation (baptism of the Holy Ghost) and as a public testimony of your faith in Jesus Christ. You have seen several examples of this on our study of Acts.

Water baptism is a **work** and **works are no longer required for salvation,** as Christ redeemed us from the curse of the Law (Gal. 3:13). Let's look at some more verses on salvation without water baptism.

"That if thou shalt confess with thy mouth the Lord Jesus, and shalt believe in thine heart that God hath raised him from the dead, thou shalt be saved. [10] For with the heart man believeth unto righteousness; and with the mouth confession is made unto salvation." (Romans 10:9-10)

Believe in your heart and confess with your mouth! No water anywhere there.

[8]"For by grace are ye saved through faith; and that not of yourselves: it is the gift of God: [9] Not of works, lest any man should boast." (Eph. 2:8-9)

Water baptism is a work, or something you have to do. As the verse says, no works are necessary!

Jesus did it all. Man has always had a problem with the simplicity of salvation and feels he has to do something himself, which is not the case. Thank God for that free gift because you couldn't do enough anyway to justify your salvation!

"Take heed therefore unto yourselves, and to all the flock, over the which the Holy Ghost hath made you overseers, to feed the church of God, which he hath purchased with his own blood." (Acts 20:28)

God purchased the Church with His own Blood. Not Blood and water! To say you have to be baptized in water is to say God's blood is not enough! Are you beginning to get the picture? Stay with us!

Chapter 4

Rightly Dividing

"Study to shew thyself approved unto God, a workman that needeth not to be ashamed, rightly dividing the word of truth." II Tim. 2:15

So, if water baptism is not nessary for salvation what is it's purpose in this present time? Should we be baptized in water or not? What about all the other verses that look like you need to be baptized to be saved? We will cover these questions in reverse order. Since we have eliminated Acts 2:38 as necessary for salvation in todays times, we still need to address some other verses which the proponents of salvation by water baptism use to prove their case.

You will quickly see that all these verses are either taken out of context, belong in another age other than the Church Age, or simply do not say what some people claim they say! So, let's examine some of these.

One verse that many use to prove water baptism is necessary for salvation is Mark 16:16. *"He that beliveth and is baptized shall be saved; but he that believeth not shall be damned."* The context of this verse (and those immediately following) is early in the apostle's ministry and prior to Pentecost as they were dealing with the Jews as in Acts 2:38. The Bible says that the Jews require a sign (I Cor. 1:22).

[17]"And these signs shall follow them that believe; In my name shall they cast out devils; they shall speak with new tongues; [18] They shall take up serpents; and if they drink any deadly thing, it shall not hurt them; they shall lay hands on the sick, and they shall recover." (Mark 16:17-18)

If you had to be baptized as in verse 16, then verses 17 and 18 should also be true. You should be able to drink any deadly thing without any ill effect and also lay hands on the sick and heal them! Don't waste your time!

The apostles lost the power of healing; also, the signs ceased when God stopped dealing with the Jew as a nation and began dealing with individuals with respect to salvation.

Put this verse in the same "no longer in effect" bag as Acts 2:38. It has no doctrinal application to salvation in this Church Age in which we now live.

Here's another good one in John 3:3-6: Jesus is telling Nicodemus, *"Except a man be born again, he cannot see the kingdom of God." [4] Nicodemus saith unto him, How can a man be born when he is old? can he enter the second time into his mother's womb, and be born?"* Jesus then explains the new birth He is talking about is a Spiritual birth and not another physical one.

[5]"...Verily, verily, I say unto thee, Except a man be born of water and of the Spirit, he cannot enter into the kingdom of God." This is not talking about water baptism. It's so simple many miss it!

Now, in verse six watch Him explain the two births mentioned in verse five: *"That which is born of the flesh is flesh; and that which is born of the Spirit is spirit."* Simple. They are two different things! A birth of the flesh and one of the Spirit.

Nicodemus is wondering how he can go back to his

mother's womb and be born again. Jesus explains in verse six that the water birth is the birth of the flesh. One is born after the mother's "water breaks," thus we all came into this world with a water birth that has nothing to do with water baptism. **Jesus is simply saying, that you need a rebirth of the Spirit, not the flesh!!**

	<u>Same</u>		<u>Same</u>
Verse 5	**water**	**&**	**Spirit**
Verse 6	**flesh**	**&**	**Spirit**

"Water" and "flesh" are the same and Spirit matches Spirit. Note the capital "S" in that verse that tells you this spiritual birth is by the Holy Spirit. *[13] "For by one Spirit are we all baptized into one body, whether we be Jews or Gentiles, whether we be bond or free; and have been all made to drink into one Spirit."* (I Cor. 12:13)

After examining these verses, it is easy to see that a verse does not always mean what it appears to say at first glance. There will be occasions, as you study your Bible, when you will find a verse that seems to contradict several other verses that all agree on a subject. In a case like this you must always believe the several verses that are plain in what they teach rather than the "odd" verse that seems to contradict.

Once the odd verses are <u>examined</u> and you determine the <u>correct context</u>, and <u>who the verse is talking to</u>, it is usually quite easy to understand. Remember God's instructions: ***"Study to shew thyself approved unto God, a workman that needeth not to be ashamed, rightly dividing the word of truth."*** (II Tim. 2:15)

Now for the best one of all! This verse is used by most who teach water baptism is necessary for salvation in the Church Age, yet we will show you where it actually teaches the opposite.

I Pet. 3:20: ***"Which sometime were disobedient, when once the longsuffering of God waited in the days of Noah, while the ark was a preparing, wherein few, that is, eight souls were saved by water. [21]The <u>like figure</u> whereunto even baptism doth also now save us (not the putting away of the filth of the flesh, but the answer of a good conscience toward God,) by the resurrection of Jesus Christ:"***

First of all, notice that the water baptism, or washing away the "filth of the flesh," does not save you, but rather it's the **"like figure" of water baptism that saves you!** The water is a "like figure" or physical picture of what happens **spiritually** when a person is saved. It pictures a death, a burial, and a ressurrection.

When you are put down into the water at baptism, it pictures the death and burial of the old man, and then when you are raised up it pictures the resurrection of the new man in Christ. (II Cor. 5:17).

After you are saved, the act of water baptism shows a good conscience toward God, and serves as a testimony of our salvation to those who are lost.

Noah is a good example. I Peter 3:20 is talking about Noah and his family. You likely know the story. The people who were in the water died lost. They received the baptism of death!

Noah and his family were saved by being "in the ark" (not the water) which is a type of you being in Jesus Christ. They were not saved by being baptized in the water! They were saved by being in the ark as you are saved by being baptized into Jesus Christ by the Holy Spirit, not being baptized in water!

We have studied the most often used verses used to promote the heresy of baptismal regeneration and have dealt with them simply by believing what we read in the proper context. **The true plan of salvation is critical if one is to be saved.** Consequently, the student must understand the importance of getting this doctrinal matter straight.

As we mentioned earlier, the Bible says in Acts 20:28 that God purchased the church (the saved body of Christ) with His own blood. It was not purchased with blood and water, but **blood alone.** You get to Heaven by trusting the shed blood of Jesus Christ and His finished work on the cross plus nothing! Not the blood plus water, or anything else, just the blood atonement alone!

To say you need anything else, especially your own works to cover your sins is a false gospel that belittles, and takes away from the sacrifice the Lord Jesus made for us.

Remember, it's trusting the finished work of Jesus Christ and His death on the cross as payment for your sins that will get you saved. Like the song says, *"It's not the water in the water main, but the blood in Emmanuel's veins"* that washes away our sins.

Consider these verses:

* **You were redeemed by the blood of Christ. (I Peter1:18-19, Col. 1:14) Not water!**

* **You are cleansed by the blood of Christ. (I John 1:7), Not water!**

* **You are made nigh to Christ by the blood. (Eph. 2: 13) Not water!**

Yes, as an act of obedience, you should be baptized in water, but only **after** you have repented, received Jesus Christ as your Saviour, and have been baptized by the Holy Spirit. Then the water baptism **pictures** your death, burial, and resurrection as a new creature in Christ.

It is also a "like figure" of that spiritual baptism, and serves as a public testimony of your new life in Christ and your commitment to Him. Trust Him, not the water, least you get baptized and go to Hell wet!

So, we have now proven, by comparing Scripture for Scripture in the correct context, and *rightly dividing the word of truth,* that water baptism is not necessary or a part of salvation in the present age in which we now live.

Rather, this heresy is in fact, a false gospel perverting the gospel of Jesus Christ and is under a curse! *[6]"I marvel that ye are so soon removed from him that called you into the grace of Christ unto another gospel: [7] Which is not another; but there be some that trouble you, and would pervert the gospel of Christ. [8] But though we, or an angel from heaven, preach any other gospel unto you than that which we have preached unto you, let him be accursed. [9] As we said before, so say I now again, If any man preach any other gospel unto you than that ye have received, let him be accursed."* (Gal 1:6-9)

At this point I believe I can safely say that no one desiring to be saved would want to mistakenly trust a false gospel for their salvation after reading these verses. So, obviously it would be expedient for us to determine what the Bible says the saving gospel of Jesus Christ is!

[1]"Moreover, brethren, I declare unto you the gospel which I preached unto you, which also ye have received, and wherein ye stand; [2] By which also ye are saved, if ye keep in memory what I

preached unto you, unless ye have believed in vain. [3] For I delivered unto you first of all that which I also received, how that Christ died for our sins according to the scriptures; [4] And that he was buried, and that he rose again the third day according to the scriptures:" (1 Cor. 15:1-4)

The Apostle Paul makes it abundantly clear that the saving gospel is trusting in the death, burial, and resurrection of Jesus Christ. He took your place on the cross and He died for your sins. He was buried, and was resurrected, defeating death and hell.

The gospel is not the death, burial, resurrection, <u>and water baptism.</u> Be careful about what you trust to save you! Just before He died on the cross for your sins He said *"It is finished."* There is nothing else that can be done to atone for your sins other than His sacrifice.

There is nothing else you can personally do but trust in "the shed blood of Jesus Christ" plus nothing as full payment for your sins. If you have not done that already, trusting Him and Him alone, without adding water, sacraments, trusting some church, priest, preacher or anything else, you are not saved according to the true gospel. You are trusting a gospel out of Hell propagated by Satan himself!

If that is the case I urge you to repent and trust the Lord Jesus Christ and Him alone, by prayer with a repentant heart and receive the baptism of the Holy Ghost! That's the one you need…that's the one you must have. That is the one you must not put off! Do it now!

May God bless you for seeking the truth!

BIBLE SALVATION

<u>COME NOW, JUST AS YOU ARE !!</u>

COME AS A SINNER: "Lord, I know I have sinned against you."

COME WITH A REPENTANT HEART: "Lord, the best way I know how, I now turn away from my sins ask for forgiveness and seek the righteousness of Jesus Christ."

COME RECEIVING JESUS AS YOUR LORD & SAVIOUR: "Lord, I believe in my heart, and now confess with my mouth that Jesus died for my sins, that He rose from the dead, and that His shed blood alone is ample and full payment for all my sins. On that basis, I now receive Jesus Christ as my Lord and Saviour. Thank you Lord God for saving my soul."

If you prayed that prayer and **meant it** you are saved and can know it!! The Bible says: *"That if thou shalt confess with thy mouth the Lord Jesus, and shalt believe in thine heart that God hath raised him from the dead, thou shalt be saved."*

[10] *"For with the heart man believeth unto righteousness; and with the mouth confession is made unto salvation."* (Romans 10:9-10).

You believed it and confessed Him so you are saved! Here is more assurance: *"He that hath the Son hath life; and he that hath not the Son of God hath not life. These things have I written unto you that believe on the name of the Son of God; that ye may know that ye have eternal life, and that ye may believe on the name of the Son of God"* (1John 5:12-13).

Thank God you now have His great salvation!